Living With...
Asthma

Nancy Dickmann

Consultant: Marjorie Hogan, MD

BROWN BEAR BOOKS

T0018670

Published by Brown Bear Books Ltd
4877 N. Circulo Bujia
Tucson, AZ 85718
USA

and

Studio G14, Regent Studios,
1 Thane Villas, London N7 7PH, UK

© 2023 Brown Bear Books Ltd

ISBN 978-1-78121-804-4 (library bound)
ISBN 978-1-78121-810-5 (paperback)

Library of Congress Cataloging-in-Publication Data available on request

Text: Nancy Dickmann
Consultant: Marjorie Hogan, MD, Professor of Pediatrics, University of Minnesota, Retired staff pediatrician, Hennepin Healthcare
Design Manager: Keith Davis
Children's Publisher: Anne O'Daly

Manufactured in the United States of America
CPSIA compliance information: Batch#AG/5651

Picture Credits
The photographs in this book are used by permission and through the courtesy of:

Front Cover: iStock: IPGGutenbergUKLtd;
Interior: iStock: Constantinia 14–15, Gorodenkoff 22t, Magic mine 6, Douglas Olivares 10–11, Twinsterphoto 4–5; Shutterstock: Aaron Amat 4, Pra Chid 10, Narong Jongsirikul 16–17, K2 PhotoStudio 14, Lemusique 16, lovelyday12 20, Monkey Business Images 8–9, Prostock-studio 12, 22b, VIVAL 20–21, Dafne Vos 18, WESTRSTOCK PRODUCTIONS 8, Zhenny-zhenny 18–19.

All other artwork and photography © Brown Bear Books.

t-top, r-right, l-left, c-center, b-bottom

Brown Bear Books has made every attempt to contact the copyright holder. If you have any information about omissions please contact: licensing@brownbearbooks.co.uk

Websites
The website addresses in this book were valid at the time of going to press. However, it is possible that contents or addresses may change following publication of this book. No responsibility for any such changes can be accepted by the author or the publisher. Readers should be supervised when they access the Internet.

Words in **bold** appear in the Words to Know on page 23

Contents

What Is Asthma?....................................4

How it Works 6

Who Gets Asthma? 8

Testing for Asthma.............................. 10

Triggers 12

Asthma and Allergies 14

Asthma Attacks.................................. 16

Inhalers 18

Living with Asthma 20

Activity 22

Words to Know 23

Find out More 24

Index 24

What Is Asthma?

Do you sometimes feel out of breath? Does your breathing make a whistling sound? Do you cough a lot? Does your chest ever feel tight? These may be signs of asthma.

People cough for many reasons. Coughs caused by asthma are often dry.

You have two lungs. They are in your chest. You use them to breathe. Asthma affects the lungs. It makes breathing harder. People with it often feel fine. But sometimes they struggle.

How it Works

You breathe in air. It goes through a tube. It travels to the lungs. The tube branches into smaller ones. These are called **airways**. Asthma makes them too sensitive. They get irritated easily.

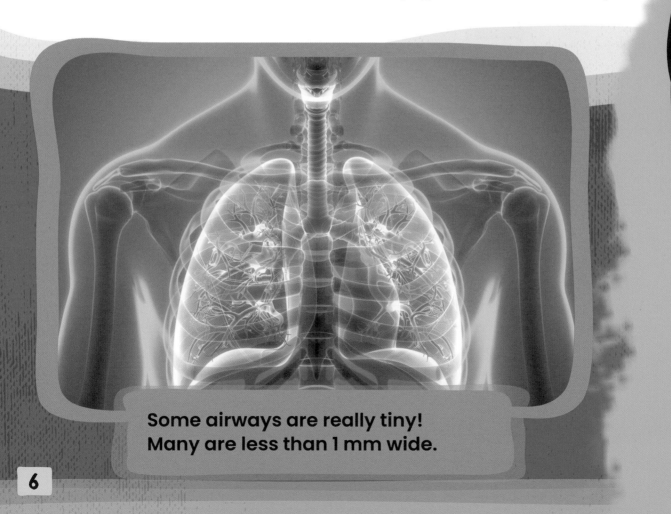

Some airways are really tiny! Many are less than 1 mm wide.

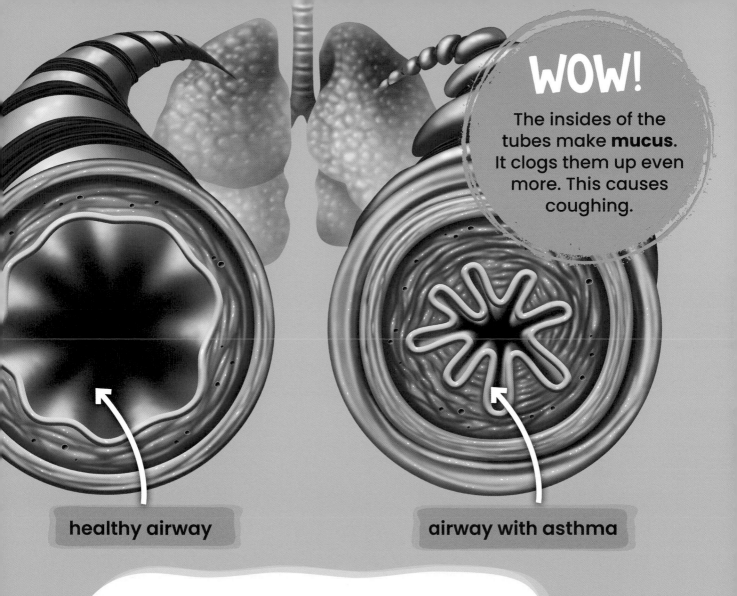

WOW!

The insides of the tubes make **mucus**. It clogs them up even more. This causes coughing.

healthy airway

airway with asthma

When this happens, their walls swell. Their muscles squeeze tighter. There is less space for air to get through. It makes a whistling sound as you breathe.

Who Gets Asthma?

Asthma is common. People of all ages have it. If often starts in childhood. Adults can get asthma too. We're not sure why some people get it and others don't.

Asthma doesn't go away. You have it for the rest of your life.

Asthma often runs in families. Some things make you more likely to get it. They are called risk factors. Allergies are one. So is being born early or too small. Breathing cigarette smoke is another.

About **25** million people in the U.S. have asthma.

That's **1** in **13** people!

Testing for Asthma

A doctor can tell if you have asthma.
They will ask about your **symptoms**.
They will ask about risk factors. If they think
you have asthma, they might do tests.

A doctor may ask you to keep
a diary. Write down when you
get any symptoms.

These tests check your breathing.
You blow into a tube or machine.
It shows how well you breathe.
Some tests are done more than once.

Kat had a cough that wouldn't go away.
She was eight years old. Doctors tested
her blood. She blew into a machine.
They found out Kat had asthma.

Triggers

Asthma symptoms come and go. People don't have them all the time. Many things can cause them. These are called **triggers**. There are lots of different ones. Everyone has their own mix.

Emotions can be a trigger. Feeling scared or worried can cause symptoms.

Common asthma triggers

- Cold weather
- Hot weather
- Storms or changes in the weather
- **Pollen** from plants
- Dust mites
- Cigarette smoke
- Air pollution
- Colds, flu, and Covid
- Damp, moldy environments
- Exercise
- Stress
- Dogs, cats, or other furry animals

Asthma and Allergies

Do you have **allergies**? Many people with asthma do. The body's defenses cause allergies. Usually they attack germs. But sometimes they get things wrong. They attack harmless things instead.

Some people are allergic to foods like nuts. Others are allergic to pollen or pets.

Some allergies make you sneeze. Others make your skin itch. Some make it hard to breathe. Any of these can also trigger asthma. This is called allergic asthma.

WOW!

Allergic asthma is very common. It makes up more than half the cases in the U.S.

Asthma Attacks

Many people live with asthma. They can manage their symptoms. But sometimes symptoms get much worse. This can build up over a few days. It can also happen suddenly. This is called an asthma attack.

Your doctor will make a plan with you. You will know what to do if you get an attack.

Asthma attacks are scary. Your chest hurts. It feels like you can't breathe. But it's important to stay calm. Ask for help. You may need to go to the hospital. The doctors there will help.

Inhalers

Most people with asthma use **inhalers**. These are tools. They have medicine inside. You breathe it in. It goes straight to your lungs. It helps open your airways.

Some inhalers have a spacer. It is a plastic tube. It helps the medicine get to your lungs.

Most people have two inhalers. One is used every day. The medicine prevents symptoms. The other is called a rescue inhaler. You use it when you get symptoms.

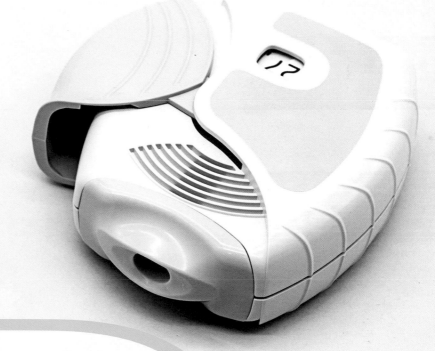

George keeps his daily inhaler next to his bed. That helps him remember to take it. He carries his rescue inhaler with him.

Living with Asthma

There are other ways to treat asthma. Some people take pills. Others get injections. Everyone's asthma is different. A doctor will work out the best plan for you.

Some people do breathing exercises. These help them relax and breathe better.

You can stay on top of your asthma. Always be prepared. Try to avoid your triggers. Staying active can help with symptoms. Asthma doesn't have to keep you from having fun!

Activity

You might not have asthma. But maybe someone you know does! You can help support them by looking out for triggers.

Take a pencil and paper and go on a trigger hunt around your home. How many can you find? Write them down.

If you know someone with asthma, ask how you can help. Make sure you know what to do if they have an asthma attack.

Words to Know

airways tubes inside your body that carry air

allergies conditions where the body's defenses attack harmless things, causing a reaction

inhaler a tool that helps a person breathe in medicine

mucus a sticky substance like snot that some body parts produce

pollen a dust-like substance made by flowers, which plants need to make seeds

symptoms the outward signs of an illness, such as a fever or rash

trigger something that sets something off or makes it happen

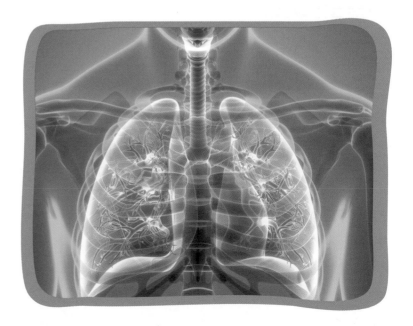

Find out More

Websites

aaaai.org/Conditions-Treatments/just-for-kids

dkfindout.com/us/human-body/lungs-and-breathing/lungs/

kidshealth.org/en/kids/asthma.html

Books

All About Asthma
Megan Borgert-Spaniol, Abdo Publications, 2019

Lungs (Human Habitats)
Robin Twiddy, Enslow Publications, 2021

Your Amazing Lungs (Your Amazing Body)
Dwayne Hicks, PowerKids Press, 2022

Index

airways 6, 7, 14, 15, 18
allergies 9
asthma attacks 16, 17

breathing 4, 5, 6, 7, 9, 11, 15, 17, 20

chest 4, 5, 17
coughing 4, 7, 11

doctors 10, 11, 16, 17, 20

inhalers 18, 19

lungs 5, 6, 18

medicine 18, 19
mucus 7

risk factors 9, 10

symptoms 10, 12, 16, 19, 21

tests 10, 11
triggers 12, 13, 15, 21

wheezing 7